Practice Book

1

CENTER STAGE

Express Yourself in English

Irene Frankel

Series Consultants

MaryAnn Florez   Sharon Seymour

PEARSON
Longman

Contents

Center Stage 1: Express Yourself in English Practice Book

Copyright © 2008 by Pearson Education, Inc.
All rights reserved.
No part of this publication may be reproduced,
stored in a retrieval system, or transmitted
in any form or by any means, electronic, mechanical,
photocopying, recording, or otherwise,
without the prior permission of the publisher.

Pearson Education, 10 Bank Street, White Plains, NY 10606

Staff credits: The people who made up the **Center Stage 1 Practice Book** team, representing editorial, production, design, and manufacturing are Pietro Alongi, Wendy Campbell, Diane Cipollone, Dave Dickey, Warren Fischbach, Aliza Greenblatt, Ray Keating, and Melissa Leyva.

Text composition: ElectraGraphics, Inc.

Text font: 9.5/11 Minion Pro

Photo credits: p. 1 (first) Kevin Peterson/AgeFotoStock, (second) Andersen Ross/AgeFotoStock, (third) Kevin Peterson/AgeFotoStock, (fourth) Amos Morgan/AgeFotoStock

Illustration credits: 101/A Corazón Abierto (Marcela Gómez), Steve Attoe, Kenneth Batelman, Marty Harris, Brian Hughes, Stephen Hutchings, Robert Kemp, Luis Monteil, Francisco Morales, Chris Pavely, Precision Graphics, Mari Rodríguez, Roberto Sadí, Gerardo Soria, John Schreiner, Gary Torrisi, Chris Vallo

ISBN-13: 978-0-13-714572-0
ISBN-10: 0-13-714572-1

Pearsonlongman on the Web
Pearsonlongman.com offers online resources for teachers and students.
Access our Companion Websites, our online catalog, and our local offices around the world.
Visit us at **pearsonlongman.com**.

Printed in the United States of America

2 3 4 5 6 7 8 9 10—VOLL—14 13 12 11

UNIT 1 VOCABULARY EXERCISES

A   Look at the pictures. Complete the information.

Manny Alba

1. ☑ Mr.   ☐ Ms.   _____Manny_____   _____Alba_____
                        (First Name)   (Last Name)

Susan Gray

2. ☐ Mr.   ☐ Ms.   _____   _____
                        (First Name)   (Family Name)

Charles Tanner

3. ☐ Mr.   ☐ Ms.   _____ , _____
                        (Last Name)   (First Name)

Grace Wong

4. ☐ Mr.   ☐ Ms.   _____ , _____
                        (Family Name)   (First Name)

B **Look at the words in the box. Then spell the names.**

Walo	~~Aziza~~	Karen
Zina	Eva	Yolanda
Jun	Ulla	Hi-won
Nadia	Lourdes	Oriana
Xan	Mpholo	Ruth
Theo	Pierre	Quincy
Ferenc	Dalal	Sun-mi
Ilhan	Victor	Carlos
Gong	Bibi	

1. A <u>z</u> <u>i</u> <u>z</u> a

2. B _ _ _ _

3. C _ r l _ _

4. D a _ _ l

5. E _ _ _

6. F _ _ e n _

7. G o _ _ _

8. H _ -w _ _ _

9. I _ _ _ n

10. J _ _ _

11. K _ _ e _

12. L _ u _ d _ _

13. M _ _ o _ o

14. N _ _ i _

15. O _ _ a _ _ _

16. P _ _ r r _

17. Q _ _ n _ _ _

18. R _ _ h

19. S _ _ - m _

20. T _ _ _ _

21. U _ l _

22. V _ c _ _ _ _

23. W _ _ o

24. X _ _ _

25. Y _ _ a _ _ _ a

26. Z _ n _

UNIT 1 GRAMMAR EXERCISES

Grammar to Communicate I:
Be: Affirmative Statements with *Am / Is*

A   Write sentences. Put the words in the correct order.

1. My name is George. _____
    (name / My / George / is)

2. _____
    (first / Maria / My / name / is)

3. _____
    (nice / meet / you / It's / to)

4. _____
    (am / Tom / Baker / I)

5. _____
    (last / My / name / Lee / is)

6. _____
    (Please / me / Nora / call)

B   Complete each sentence. Use the words in the box. Use capital letters as needed.

is   it's   'm   my   ~~name~~   nice

1. My last ___name___ is Sanchez.

2. My first name _____ Victor.

3. It's _____ to meet you, Victor.

4. I _____ Jason Smith.

5. _____ nice to meet you, Jason.

6. _____ name is Thomas Hale.

Grammar to Communicate 2:
Pronouns: *He / She*
Possessive Adjectives: *His / Her*

A **Complete each sentence. Use *He*, *She*, *His*, or *Her*.**

1. She's my teacher. _____Her_____ name is Ms. Robles.

2. _____'s Mr. Johnson. He's nice.

3. That's Tom. _____ last name is Kramer.

4. He's my teacher. _____ name is Hector Santiago.

5. _____'s my classmate. Her name is Sonia.

6. That's Ms. Jones. _____ first name is Alexa.

B **Match the questions with the answers. Write the correct letters.**

___d___ 1. Who's that?   **a.** H-I-R-S-C-H.

_____ 2. What's your last name?   **b.** Her first name is Linda.

_____ 3. What's his last name?   **c.** His last name is Hirsch.

_____ 4. Could you spell that, please?   **d.** That's my teacher.

_____ 5. What's her first name?   **e.** My last name is Santos.

Review

Put the conversation in order. Write the sentences on the lines.

Franklin. Jim Franklin. It's nice to meet you, Ms. Green.

~~Hi. I'm Jim Franklin.~~

And please call me Jim.

It's nice to meet you, Mr. Franklin. And please call me Beth.

Hello. My name is Beth Green. What's your last name again?

A: Hi. I'm Jim Franklin. _____

_____

B: _____

_____

A: _____

_____

B: _____

_____

A: _____

_____

UNIT 2 VOCABULARY EXERCISES

 A Look at the maps. Write the names of the countries. Use the words in the boxes.

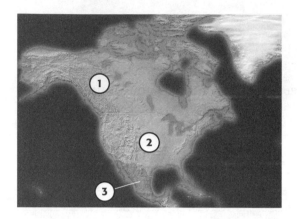

| Canada   Mexico   ~~the United States~~ |

1. _____   3. _____

2. _____the United States_____

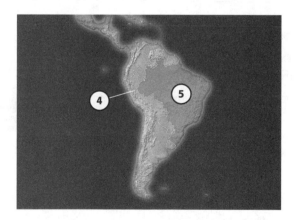

| Brazil   Peru |

4. _____   5. _____

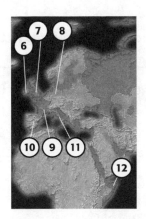

| England | France | Germany | Italy | Ireland | Somalia | Spain |

6. _____   10. _____

7. _____   11. _____

8. _____   12. _____

9. _____

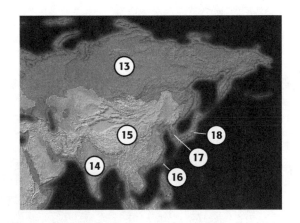

| China | India | Japan | Korea | Russia | Taiwan |

13. _____   16. _____

14. _____   17. _____

15. _____   18. _____

B   **Complete each sentence. Use the words in the box.**

American	German	Korean
British	Italian	Mexican
Chinese	Japanese	Spanish

(American is crossed out in the box)

1. Nancy is from the U.S. She's ___American___ .

2. Lourdes is from Spain. She's _____ .

3. Eriko is from Japan. She's _____ .

4. Sofia is from Italy. She's _____ .

5. Xan is from China. He's _____ .

6. Ernesto is from Mexico. He's _____ .

7. Tom is from England. He's _____ .

8. Gisela is from Germany. She's _____ .

9. Jun is from Korea. He's _____ .

UNIT 2 GRAMMAR EXERCISES

Grammar to Communicate 1:
Be: Statements

A **Rewrite each sentence. Use contractions.**

1. He is nice.   He's nice. _____

2. I am Alfredo.   _____

3. He is my teacher.   _____

4. She is cute.   _____

5. They are from France.   _____

6. We are from Taiwan.   _____

7. You are from the U.S.   _____

8. It is Italian.   _____

B **Rewrite each sentence. Use the negative.**

1. He's from Mexico.   He's not from Mexico. _____

2. Anna is from Germany.   _____

3. Mr. Solomon is from Canada. _____

4. We are from Italy.   _____

5. They are from India.   _____

6. Tacos are from Brazil.   _____

Grammar to Communicate 2:
Be: Yes / No Questions and Short Answers

A **Complete the conversations. Use the questions in the box.**

Are Sara and Maria from Spain?	Are you Canadian?	Is he British?
Are they Japanese?	Are you French?	~~Is he Russian?~~

1. **A:** Is he Russian?

   B: Yes, he is. He's from Moscow.

2. **A:** _____

   B: No, I'm not French. I'm American.

3. **A:** _____

   B: Yes, they are. They're from Tokyo.

4. **A:** _____

   B: Yes, we are. We're from Toronto.

5. **A:** _____

   B: No, he isn't. He's from India.

6. **A:** _____

   B: No, they aren't. They're from Peru.

B **Write sentences. Put the words in the correct order. Use contractions.**

1. Ms. Kyo isn't from Korea.
   (Ms. Kyo / Korea / from / not / is)

2. _____
   (British / Jack and Sam / not / are)

3. _____
   (from / Lucy / is / not / Canada)

4. _____
   (The teacher / not / Japanese / is)

5. _____
   (am / from / I / not / France)

6. _____
   (India / from / not / Wendy and I / are)

Review

Complete the conversation. Use the words in the box. You may use a word more than one time. Use capital letters as needed.

are	aren't	is	isn't	they're

A: _____Are_____ hamburgers American?

B: No, they _____. They're German.

A: _____ French fries American?

B: No, they aren't. _____ from Belgium.

A: Is spaghetti American?

B: No, it _____. It's Italian.

A: _____ fried chicken American?

B: Yes, it _____.

UNIT 3 VOCABULARY EXERCISES

A   Look at the picture. Who is in the family? Read each question. Write the numbers you see in the picture.

1. Who is the grandfather?   ____1____

2. Who is the mother?   _____

3. Who is the sister?   _____

4. Who is the grandmother?   _____

5. Who are the parents?   _____

6. Who are the grandparents?   _____

7. Who are the sister and brother?   _____

8. Who is the father?   _____

9. Who is the brother?   _____

B **Write the numbers.**

1. eighteen = __18__

2. nine = _____

3. eleven = _____

4. two = _____

5. ten = _____

6. twelve = _____

7. thirteen = _____

8. four = _____

9. five = _____

10. zero = _____

11. three = _____

12. one = _____

13. fourteen = _____

14. eight = _____

15. sixteen = _____

16. seven = _____

17. nineteen = _____

18. seventeen = _____

19. six = _____

20. fifteen = _____

UNIT 3 GRAMMAR EXERCISES

Grammar to Communicate I:
A / An with Singular Nouns

A   CompleteComplete each sentence. Use *a* or *an*.

1. My brother Sam is _____*a*_____ teacher.

2. My father is _____ doctor.

3. Mr. Gomez is _____ engineer.

4. Mrs. Shields is _____ bus driver.

5. Barry is _____ lawyer.

6. His sister is _____ artist.

B   CompleteComplete the conversations. Circle the correct answers.

1. **A:** Is he **a** / **an** engineer?

   B: No, he isn't. He's **a** / **an** teacher.

2. **A:** Are you **a** / **an** painter?

   B: No, I'm not. I'm **a** / **an** mechanic.

3. **A:** Is your sister **a** / **an** homemaker?

   B: No, she isn't. She's **a** / **an** lawyer.

4. **A:** Are you **a** / **an** salesperson?

   B: No, I'm not. I'm **a** / **an** assistant.

5. **A:** Is his mother **a** / **an** doctor?

   B: No, she isn't. She's **a** / **an** dentist.

6. **A:** Are you **a** / **an** English student?

   B: No, I'm not. I'm **a** / **an** English teacher.

Grammar to Communicate 2:
Be: Information Questions

A   **Match the questions with the answers. Write the correct letters.**

_c_ **1.** Where are you from?   **a.** He's in San Antonio.

____ **2.** How old is she?   **b.** I'm 15.

____ **3.** Who's he?   **c.** I'm from Italy.

____ **4.** Where is your father?   **d.** He's my grandfather.

____ **5.** How old are you?   **e.** She's 10.

____ **6.** What's his name?   **f.** His name is Emilio.

B   **Read the answers. Complete each question. Use *What*, *Where*, *Who*, or *How old*.**

1. A: _____Who_____ is he?

    B: He's my father.

2. A: _____ is she from?

    B: She's from Japan.

3. A: _____'s her name?

    B: Her name is Akiko.

4. A: _____ is he?

    B: He's 12.

5. A: _____ are they?

    B: They're in Chicago.

6. A: _____'s that woman?

    B: That's my friend Ruth.

Review

Look at the picture. Complete the conversation. Use the words in the box. You may use a word more than one time.

a	an	How old	What's	Where	Who's

A: Is this your family?

B: Yes, it is.

A: ___Who's___ he?

B: He's my grandfather. He's _____ engineer.

A: _____ his name?

B: His name is Thomas.

A: _____ is he from?

B: He's from Cuba.

A: _____ he?

B: He's my brother. He's _____ student.

A: _____ his name?

B: His name is Alex.

A: _____ is he?

B: He's 16.

NAME: _____   DATE: _____

UNIT 4 VOCABULARY EXERCISES

A Read the information about Karen, Victor, and Sun-mi. Then complete the information in the box.

Karen Blake	Victor Santiago	Sun-mi Lee
233 Green Street	200 Roberts Avenue	9 Court Street
New York, NY 10001	Chicago, IL 60611	Boston, MA 02144
212-555-9425	804-555-2006	617-555-8989
kblake@coolmail.com	VicSan@coolmail.com	FunSun28@coolmail.com

CONTACT INFORMATION		
Name	**Phone Number**	**E-mail Address**
Karen Blake	1. 212-555-9425	2.
Victor Santiago	3.	4.
Sun-mi Lee	5.	6.

B Write the numbers.

1. forty-two = ___42___

2. fifty-three = _____

3. twenty-four = _____

4. ninety-nine = _____

5. eighty-five = _____

6. twenty-one = _____

7. thirty-eight = _____

8. sixty-seven = _____

9. a hundred = _____

10. thirty-nine = _____

11. twenty-two = _____

12. seventy-five = _____

13. forty = _____

14. sixty-eight = _____

15. seventy-six = _____

16. ninety-four = _____

17. eighty-three = _____

18. fifty-seven = _____

UNIT 4 GRAMMAR EXERCISES

Grammar to Communicate 1:
Possessive Adjectives

A **Complete each sentence. Use *our*, *your*, and *their*. Use capital letters as needed.**

1. My husband and I are in the U.S. _____Our_____ parents are in Korea.

2. They're students. Ms. Vlahos is _____ teacher.

3. They're my children. _____ names are Sara and Kyle.

4. My sister and I are students. _____ mother is a student, too.

5. You and your friend are in English 1. _____ class is Room 632.

6. My brother is in California. _____ parents are there, too.

B **Complete each sentence. Use the correct possessive adjective *My*, *Your*, *His*, *Her*, *Our*, or *Their*.**

1. I'm Tom Hayes. _____My_____ name is Tom Hayes.

2. She's Dolores Rios. _____ phone number is 555-7834.

3. We're from Florida. _____ address is 38 Ocean Drive, Miami, Florida.

4. You're Bridget. _____ last name is Kane.

5. He's Ray Tapa. _____ last name is Tapa.

6. They're students. _____ names are Shu and Ito.

Grammar to Communicate 2:
Possessive Nouns

A Write each sentence. Use a possessive noun and a form of *be*.

1. Diego / address / 325 Cherry Street

   Diego's address is 325 Cherry Street.

2. Mr. Robertson / cell phone number / 917-555-5993

   _____

3. Cindy / phone number / 555-3327

   _____

4. Mr. and Mrs. Mason / address / 5490 Port Boulevard

   _____

5. My brother / e-mail address / gosporty@online.net

   _____

6. Tanya / address / 320 Court Street

   _____

B Rewrite each sentence in Exercise A. Change the possessive nouns to possessive pronouns.

1. *His address is 325 Cherry Street.*

2. _____

3. _____

4. _____

5. _____

6. _____

Review

Look at the chart. Complete the conversation.

NAME	ADDRESS	PHONE NUMBER
Nora Tine	749 Brighton Avenue	555-7878
Sam Baer	32 Plainfield Road	555-9652
Bob Kane	3056 Ocean Boulevard	555-6673
Julie Caruso	284 Rockville Street	555-6194

A: What's _____Nora Tine's_____ phone number?

B: It's 555-7878.

A: What's her _____?

B: It's 749 Brighton Avenue.

A: What's _____ address?

B: It's 32 Plainfield Road.

A: What's _____ phone number?

B: It's 555-6673.

A: What's his address?

B: It's _____.

A: What's Julie Caruso's _____?

B: It's 284 Rockville Street.

A: What's _____ phone number?

B: It's _____.

UNIT 5 VOCABULARY EXERCISES

A Look at the picture. Write the words on the lines. Use the words in the box.

backpack	box of chalk	dictionary	glasses	pencil
~~board~~	chair	door	notebook	window
book	closet	eraser	pen	workbook
bookcase	desk	notebook		

1. _____board_____   7. _____   13. _____

2. _____   8. _____   14. _____

3. _____   9. _____   15. _____

4. _____   10. _____   16. _____

5. _____   11. _____   17. _____

6. _____   12. _____

B Look at the pictures. Complete each sentence. Circle the letter of the correct answer.

1. The chalk is _____ the book.

   a. on   **b.** in

2. The chalk is _____ the box.

   a. near   **b.** in

3. The pens and pencils are _____ the chalk.

   a. near   **b.** on

C Complete each sentence. Circle the correct answer. Write it on the line.

1. _____*Take out*_____ a piece of paper.
   (Take out / Write)

2. _____ your hand.
   (Listen to / Raise)

3. _____ the window.
   (Use / Open)

4. _____ the board.
   (Erase / Close)

5. _____ a pen.
   (Use / Write)

6. _____ a sentence aloud.
   (Point to / Read)

7. _____ the CD.
   (Turn to / Listen to)

8. _____ your answers.
   (Write / Take out)

9. _____ the door.
   (Listen to / Close)

10. _____ page 23.
    (Turn to / Erase)

11. _____ the picture.
    (Point to / Use)

12. _____ the board.
    (Raise / Look at)

UNIT 5 GRAMMAR EXERCISES

Grammar to Communicate 1: Plural of Regular Nouns

A **Rewrite each sentence. Change the underlined words to the plural. Make all necessary changes.**

1. The <u>book</u> is on the desk.   *The books are on the desk.*

2. The <u>pen</u> is on the bookcase.   _____

3. His <u>notebook</u> is in his backpack. _____

4. The <u>closet</u> is near the door.   _____

5. Their <u>dictionary</u> is on the chair. _____

6. The <u>eraser</u> is near the board.   _____

B **Complete each conversation. Circle the correct answer.**

1. A: Where's my **notebook** / **notebooks**?

    B: It's on the desk.

2. A: Where are the **dictionary** / **dictionaries**?

    B: They're in the bookcase.

3. A: Where's the **box** / **boxes** of chalk?

    B: It's near the board.

4. A: Where's his **backpack** / **backpack**?

    B: It's on the chair.

5. A: Where are the **workbook** / **workbooks**?

    B: They're in the closet.

6. A: Where's your **pen** / **pens**?

    B: It's on my desk.

Grammar to Communicate 2:
Imperatives

A **Complete each sentence. Use the words in the box.**

listen to	~~look at~~	open	raise	take out	turn to	write

1. Please ____look at____ the board.

2. Don't _____ in your books.

3. Carlos, please _____ the window.

4. Please _____ your hand.

5. Don't talk. Please _____ your teacher.

6. Please _____ page 22 in your workbooks.

7. Anita, please _____ a piece of paper.

B **Rewrite each sentence. Change the affirmative imperatives to negative and the negative imperatives to affirmative.**

1. Don't use a pen on the test.   _Use a pen on the test._____

2. Erase the board, please.   _____

3. Close the door.   _____

4. Don't write your answers on the paper.   _____

5. Please don't look at your book.   _____

6. Don't listen to me, please.   _____

NAME: _____   DATE: _____

Review

Look at the list of rules. Write negative or affirmative imperative sentences.

TEST RULES

✓ use a pen	✓ read all the instructions
✗ use a pencil	✓ print your name on the test
✗ open your books	✗ stand up
✓ write on the answer sheet	✗ write on the test
✓ sign the test	✗ talk

1. Use a pen.

2. Don't use a pencil.

3. _____

4. _____

5. _____

6. _____

7. _____

8. _____

9. _____

10. _____

UNIT 6 VOCABULARY EXERCISES

 A Look at the pictures. Complete each sentence. Use the words in the boxes.

cool	~~hot~~

1. It's ____hot____ .   2. It's not _____ .

rainy	sunny

3. It's _____ .   4. It's not _____ .

foggy	snowy

5. It's _____ .   6. It's not _____ .

cloudy	windy

7. It's _____.

8. It's not _____.

cold	warm

9. It's _____.

10. It's not _____.

B Write the days of the week in the calendar. Use the words in the box.

Friday	Monday	Saturday	~~Sunday~~	Thursday	Tuesday	Wednesday

January						
1. Sunday	**2.** _____	**3.** _____	**4.** _____	**5.** _____	**6.** _____	**7.** _____
1	2 9:00 English	3 9:00 English	4 9:00 English 3:00 Doctor	5 9:00 English	6 9:00 English 6:00 Dinner with Hiro	7 8:30 Party!

C **Read the calendar in Exercise B again. Circle the correct answer. Write it on the line.**

1. English class is at nine _____ o'clock _____.
   (**o'clock** / clock)

2. English class is in the _____.
   (afternoon / morning)

3. Dinner with Hiro is in the _____.
   (morning / evening)

4. I am at the doctor's office on Wednesday _____.
   (afternoon / night)

5. My party is on Saturday _____.
   (morning / night)

6. 12:00 A.M. is _____.
   (noon / midnight)

7. 12:00 P.M. is _____.
   (noon / midnight)

NAME: _____ DATE: _____

UNIT 6 GRAMMAR EXERCISES

Grammar to Communicate 1:
Be: Information Questions

 A Look at the chart. Read each sentence. What day is it? Write a sentence about the correct day.

Monday	Tuesday	Wednesday	Thursday	Friday	Saturday
sunny	rainy	cloudy	sunny	sunny	cloudy
85°	70°	75°	90°	95°	80°

1. It's sunny. It's 85°. <u>It's Monday.</u>

2. It's sunny. It's 90°. _____

3. It's rainy. It's 70°. _____

4. It's sunny. It's 95°. _____

5. It's cloudy. It's 75°. _____

6. It's cloudy. It's 80°. _____

B Match the questions with the answers. Write the correct letters.

__c__ 1. What day is today?   **a.** Yes, it is. It's 92°.

_____ 2. What's the weather?   **b.** It's 78°.

_____ 3. What's the temperature?   **c.** It's Wednesday.

_____ 4. Is it cold today?   **d.** No, it isn't. It's warm.

_____ 5. Is it hot today?   **e.** It's cloudy and cool.

_____ 6. Is it sunny today?   **f.** No, it isn't. It's cloudy.

Grammar to Communicate 2:
Be: Information Questions

A **Complete each sentence. Use *at*, *in*, *on*, and *to*.**

1. My class is _____*on*_____ Monday.

2. His test is _____ 6:00.

3. Their classes are _____ the morning, from 9:00 _____ noon.

4. The school is open _____ Saturday.

5. Her English class is _____ 7:00 _____ night.

B **Complete each conversation. Write the questions. Put the words in the correct order.**

1. **A:** _What time is it?_____
       (it / is / time / What)

    B: It's 10:30.

2. **A:** _____
       (your / are / What / work hours)

    B: From 3:00 to 7:00, Monday to Wednesday.

3. **A:** _____
       (their / is / class / When)

    B: It's on Tuesday and Thursday.

4. **A:** _____
       (test / When / the / is)

    B: It's on Wednesday.

5. **A:** _____
       (class / What / his / time / is)

    B: It's at 4:00 in the afternoon.

6. **A:** _____
       (What / lunch / time / is)

    B: It's at 12:30.

7. **A:** _____
       (the / are / office / What / hours)

    B: They're 9:00 to 5:00, Monday to Thursday.

Review

Read the answers. Then complete each question. Use the words in the box and 's, is, or are. You will use some words more than one time.

What	What day	What time	When

1. A: ___What's___ the weather today?   B: It's sunny and hot.

2. A: _____ the temperature?   B: It's 80°.

3. A: _____ your work hours?   B: From 4:00 to 10:00 P.M.

4. A: _____ your class?   B: It's on Saturday morning.

5. A: _____ your test?   B: It's at 8:30.

6. A: _____ today?   B: It's Tuesday.

7. A: _____ your classes?   B: On Tuesday and Thursday.

NAME: _____   DATE: _____

UNIT 7 VOCABULARY EXERCISES

 A   **Look at the pictures. Circle the clothes you see. You may circle more than one word.**

1.

(coat)   socks   T-shirt

2.

dress   pants   shoes

3.

pants   sweater   tie

4.

blouse   jacket   suit

5.

blouse   jeans   skirt

6.

polo shirt   suit   tie

7.

pants   sneakers   T-shirt

8.

jeans   polo shirt   skirt

B Look at the words in the box. Then unscramble the words in parentheses. Complete each sentence. Write the correct words on the lines. You may use a word more than once.

beige	brown	large	purple	white
black	extra large	medium	red	yellow
blue	green	orange	small	

1. The Japanese flag is ____red____ and _____.
   (edr)   (heiwt)

2. The German flag is _____, _____, and _____.
   (kcbla)   (rde)   (lweoly)

3. The Italian flag is _____, _____, and _____.
   (neerg)   (tiehw)   (der)

4. The American flag is _____, _____, and _____.
   (rde)   (ietwh)   (lebu)

5. Her sneakers are _____ and _____.
   (gareno)   (lerppu)

6. His tie is _____ and _____.
   (geebi)   (wonrb)

7. This blouse is big. It's _____.
   (realg)

8. This blouse is not big. It's _____.
   (laslm)

9. This blouse is very big. It's _____.
   (txrea glera)

10. This blouse is not big or small. It's _____.
    (idmume)

NAME: _____ DATE: _____

UNIT 7 GRAMMAR EXERCISES

Grammar to Communicate 1:
Demonstrative Adjectives: *This / That / These / Those*

 A   **Complete each conversation. Circle the correct answers.**

1. **A:** Elena, look at (that)/ **those** sweater. It's beautiful!

   B: Yes, it is. And look at **that / those** jeans. They're nice.

2. **A:** **This / These** shirt isn't my size.

   B: Look at **this / these** shirts. They're on sale.

3. **A:** Are the pants on sale?

   B: **This / These** pants are on sale, but **that / those** pants aren't.

4. **A:** **This / These** skirt is nice.

   B: Yes, but **that / those** skirt over there is on sale.

5. **A:** Look at **this / these** blouse! It's only $12.99.

   B: **That / Those** blouses are on sale, too.

B   **Look at the pictures. Complete the sentences with *this*, *that*, *these*, or *those*. Use capital letters as needed.**

1. Are ____*these*____ shirts on sale?   2. _____ socks are nice.

3. _____ jacket isn't expensive.   4. Is _____ T-shirt nice?

Grammar to Communicate 2:
Questions with *How Much*
Questions with *What Color*

A   Complete each question. Use *How much is* or *How much are*.

1. **A:** _____How much is_____ this tie?
   B: It's $29.95.

2. **A:** _____ these jeans?
   B: They're $59.00.

3. **A:** _____ those
   sneakers?
   B: They're $75.00.

4. **A:** _____ this jacket?
   B: It's $98.00.

5. **A:** _____ that
   polo shirt?
   B: It's $30.00.

6. **A:** _____
   those coats?
   B: They're $79.99.

7. **A:** _____ that
   skirt?
   B: It's $19.95.

B   Look at the picture. Complete each conversation.

1. **A:** _____What color is_____ the shirt?
   B: It's green.
   A: _____ it?
   B: It's $19.95.

2. **A:** _____ the socks?
   B: _____ red.
   A: _____ they?
   B: They're $ _____.

3. **A:** _____ the
   sweater?
   B: _____ blue.
   A: _____ it?
   B: _____ $34.99.

Review

Complete the conversation. Use the questions in the box.

~~Are they on sale?~~	How much are they?	What color are they?
Are those pants on sale, too?	How much is this sweater?	

A: Oh, look at these sweaters.

B: They're nice.

A: *Are they on sale?*

B: Yes, they are. Buy one, get one free.

A: _____

B: It's $24.99.

A: That's a great price. _____

B: No, those pants aren't on sale. But these pants are on sale.

A: _____

B: They're $39.99.

A: That's good. _____

B: They're green, black, and beige.

UNIT 8 VOCABULARY EXERCISES

A **Complete the conversation. Circle the correct answer. Write it on the line.**

Jimmy: Mom, where is my book?

Mom: Look in the closet in the _____ *hall* _____.
1. (hall / window)

Jimmy: It's not there.

Dad: Look on the bookcase in the _____.
2. (bathroom / living room)

Jimmy: No, it's not there.

Mom: Hmm . . . Where is it?

Gina: I think it's next to the bed in the _____.
3. (children's bedroom / kitchen)

Mom: No . . . it's not there.

Grandpa: Is it next to the _____ in the window?
4. (blinds / carpeting)

Jimmy: No!

Grandma: Well, look next to your chair in the _____.
5. (hall / dining room)

Jimmy: It's not there.

Dad: Look in the _____, next to my coffee.
6. (bathroom / kitchen)

Jimmy: It's not there.

Grandpa: Look in your mother's room.

Jimmy: No, it's not in my _____ bedroom.
7. (children's / parents')

Grandma: Is it next to the sink in the _____.
8. (bathroom / air-conditioning)

Jimmy: No.

Mom: Well, look in the . . .

Jimmy: Oh, here it is!

Dad: Where?

Jimmy: It's in my backpack!

B **Look at the picture. Read each sentence. For each sentence, write _T_ for _True_ or _F_ for _False_.**

1. The refrigerator is next to the dishwasher. _____

2. The microwave is on the table. _____

3. The freezer is next to the stove. _____

4. The dryer is over the washing machine. _____

5. The chairs are on the counter. _____

6. The curtains are in the cabinets. _____

7. The washing machine is under the dryer. _____

8. The sink is next to the dishwasher. _____

UNIT 8 GRAMMAR EXERCISES

Grammar to Communicate 1:
There Is / There Are: Statements

A Complete the e-mail. Use *there's* or *there are*. Use capital letters as needed.

Dear Jack,

My sister's new apartment is very nice. ___There's___ a large kitchen, and

it's very sunny. _____ two large bedrooms and one small bedroom.

_____ no closets in the small bedroom. _____ a nice living

room and a small dining room. _____ no carpeting, but _____

blinds on all the windows. _____ two bathrooms. _____

one bathroom in the hall, and _____ a bathroom in a bedroom.

_____ no air-conditioning, but _____ seven windows.

Love,
Lucy

B Read the list. Then correct the mistake in each sentence. Write a correct sentence.

Lakeview apartment

2 bedrooms	✗ air-conditioning
✓ kitchen	✓ living room
2 closets	✗ dining room
✓ carpeting	a lot of windows

1. There's no kitchen.   There's a kitchen. _____

2. There are no closets.   _____

3. There are no windows.   _____

4. There are three bedrooms.   _____

5. There's no carpeting.   _____

6. There's a dining room.   _____

7. There's air-conditioning.   _____

8. There's no living room.   _____

Grammar to Communicate 2
There Is / There Are: Yes / No Questions and Short Answers

A Rewrite each sentence. Change the statements to questions.

1. There are cabinets over the sink.   *Are there any cabinets over the sink?*

2. There's a window in the kitchen.   _____

3. There's a microwave on the counter.   _____

4. There are curtains on the windows.   _____

5. There are cabinets over the stove.   _____

6. There's a table in the kitchen.   _____

7. There are chairs in the kitchen.   _____

B Complete the conversation. Use *there is* and *there are*. Use capital letters as needed.

A: Is there a big kitchen in your new apartment?

B: Yes, ___*there is*___. And there's a table and four chairs.

A: Is there a window in the kitchen?

B: Yes, _____.

A: Are there any closets?

B: Yes, _____. There are three closets.

A: Are there any cabinets in the kitchen?

B: Yes, _____. There are a lot of cabinets.

A: What about the bedrooms?

B: _____ three bedrooms.

A: Is there air-conditioning?

B: No, _____.

A: Is there carpeting?

B: Yes, _____. There's nice blue carpeting in the living room and hall.

NAME: _____ DATE: _____

Review

Read the ad. Complete the conversation.

> **FOR RENT:** 3BR apt. Modern kitchen w/
> a lot of cabinets. New stove, refrigerator,
> microwave. W/D in hall. 5 closets. 2 BTH.
> Large, sunny LR w/ Dining area. 7 windows.

A: So, how's the apartment?

B: It's great. I really like it!

A: _Are there_ any closets?

B: Yes, _____.

A: How's the kitchen?

B: It's very modern. There are a lot of _____.

A: _____ a microwave?

B: _____. And the stove and refrigerator are new.

A: Oh, that's great. Anything else?

B: _____ a washing machine and dryer in the hall.

A: Is there a dining room?

B: _____. But _____ a dining area in the living room.

A: That's great! And what about bathrooms?

B: There are _____ bathrooms.

A: And the bedrooms?

B: That's the best part. _____ three bedrooms.

A: It sounds like the perfect apartment.

UNIT 9 VOCABULARY EXERCISES

A   **Complete each sentence. Circle the letter of the correct answer.**

1. Eat soup with a _____.

    a. fork   **(b.)** spoon

2. Eat cake with a _____.

    a. fork   **b.** knife

3. Don't eat soup with a _____.

    a. knife   **b.** spoon

4. This _____ is hot!

    a. salad   **b.** tomato soup

5. There's _____ for dessert.

    a. apple pie and chocolate cake   **b.** tuna salad and tomato soup

6. I want a turkey sandwich with _____ on it.

    a. grilled chicken   **b.** Swiss cheese

7. I like egg _____ sandwiches.

    a. salad   **b.** soup

B   **Match the words with the pictures. Write the correct letters.**

_____ **1.** turkey   **a.**

_____ **2.** tuna salad   **b.**

_____ **3.** grilled chicken   **c.**

C **Read each sentence. Complete each sentence. Use the words in the boxes.**

check	~~coffee~~	hot chocolate	juice	milk	salt	water

1. It's a hot drink. It's black. I drink it at breakfast. It's ____coffee____.

2. This cold drink is white. It's _____.

3. This drink is cold. It's from fruits or vegetables. It's _____.

4. This drink is brown. It has hot milk and sugar. It's _____.

5. I'm thirsty. I want a glass of _____.

6. It's white. It's not sugar. It's next to the pepper. It's _____.

7. Waiters write your order on this. It's a _____.

glass	iced tea	napkin	pepper	soda	sugar	tea

8. It's a hot drink. It's brown. It's _____.

9. It's a cold drink. It's brown. It's _____.

10. It's white. It's in cake. It's _____.

11. Coke and Pepsi are kinds of _____.

12. I like a _____ of water with dinner.

13. It's black. It's next to the salt. It's _____.

14. It's next to the fork. It's paper. It's a _____.

UNIT 9 GRAMMAR EXERCISES

Grammar to Communicate 1:
Simple Present: Affirmative Statements with *Want, Like, Need*

A   Complete each sentence. Use the correct form of the verbs in parentheses.

1. My sister _____ *likes* _____ tomato soup.
       (like)

2. They _____ chocolate ice cream.
          (want)

3. I _____ turkey sandwiches.
       (like)

4. Jason _____ a spoon.
            (need)

5. Mr. and Mrs. Thomson _____ forks.
                            (need)

6. My mother _____ soup.
                  (want)

B   Look at the lunch order. Write sentences about the people. Use *want* or *wants*.

Zack	a tuna salad sandwich
Liana	a Swiss cheese sandwich
Terry and Chris	grilled chicken sandwiches
Mr. Oakes	a salad
Mindy and Carol	tomato soup
Michelle	a hamburger

1. Zack wants a tuna salad sandwich. _____

2. _____

3. _____

4. _____

5. _____

6. _____

Grammar to Communicate 2:
Simple Present: Negative Statements with *Want, Like, Need*

A   Complete each sentence. Use *don't* or *doesn't* and the verbs in parentheses.

1. Cara _____*doesn't want*_____ milk in her coffee.
      (want)

2. I _____ sugar, thanks.
      (need)

3. She _____ soda, but she likes juice.
      (like)

4. Allie _____ iced tea.
      (want)

5. Sheila and Mary _____ napkins.
      (need)

6. We _____ soda with our sandwiches.
      (like)

B   Complete each sentence. Write the negative form of the underlined verbs.

1. He <u>likes</u> turkey. He _____*doesn't like*_____ chicken.

2. Mara <u>wants</u> apple pie. She _____ ice cream.

3. They <u>need</u> forks. They _____ spoons.

4. I <u>like</u> chicken soup. I _____ tomato soup.

5. You <u>need</u> more coffee. You _____ milk.

6. The children <u>like</u> egg salad. They _____ tuna salad.

7. We <u>want</u> more salad. We _____ more chicken.

8. Mr. Ito <u>likes</u> hot tea. He _____ iced tea.

NAME: _____   DATE: _____

Review

Write sentences. Put the words in the correct order.

1. _Bob doesn't like milk in his coffee._
   (Bob / in his coffee / like / milk / doesn't)

2. _____
   (Our teacher / salt / for his hamburger / needs)

3. _____
   (She / want / with her lunch / doesn't / a salad)

4. _____
   (My children / for dessert / chocolate ice cream / like)

5. _____
   (Dave and Irene / want / more coffee / don't)

6. _____
   (Mr. Davos / sandwich / and / wants / a / soup / grilled chicken)

NAME: _____   DATE: _____

UNIT 10 VOCABULARY EXERCISES

A **Match the sentences. Write the correct letters.**

THE PATIENT . . .

  _b_ **1.** I'm hot.

_____ **2.** I have a headache.

_____ **3.** My throat is red.

_____ **4.** Aaachoo! I have a cold.

_____ **5.** I'm hot and cold and hot and cold.

THE DOCTOR . . .

a. You have the flu.

b. You have a fever.

c. You have a sore throat.

d. You need chicken soup.

e. You need an aspirin.

B **Match the sentences with the pictures. Write the correct letters.**

a.

b.

c.

d.

e.

_____ **1.** I have an earache.

_____ **2.** I have a backache.

_____ **3.** I have a cough.

_____ **4.** I have a pain.

_____ **5.** I have a stomachache.

C **Match the sentences. Write the correct letters.**

YOU . . .

_____ 1. I'm hungry.

_____ 2. I'm cold.

_____ 3. I'm tired.

_____ 4. I'm thirsty.

_____ 5. I'm hot.

_____ 6. I'm sick.

_____ 7. I'm dizzy.

_____ 8. I'm nauseous.

_____ 9. I'm better.

YOUR FRIEND . . .

a. Here's a glass of water.

b. Here's a sweater.

c. That's good!

d. Go to bed.

e. Go to the doctor.

f. Here's a sandwich.

g. You have a fever.

h. Sit down!

i. Don't eat.

UNIT 10 GRAMMAR EXERCISES

Grammar to Communicate 1:
Simple Present: Statements with *Have*

A Complete each sentence. Use *has* or *have*.

1. Sara isn't in class today. She ____has____ the flu.

2. I'm sick. I _____ a fever.

3. Her children aren't in school today. They _____ colds.

4. I don't want a sandwich. I _____ a stomachache.

5. Mr. Hobbs isn't here today. He _____ a backache.

6. We're sick. We _____ the flu.

7. Ms. Ardano needs aspirin. She _____ a headache.

B Look at each picture. Then complete each sentence. Use *has* or *doesn't have*.

1. He __doesn't have__ a cough. He ____has____ an earache.

2. He _____ a sore throat. He _____ a backache.

3. She _____ a cold. She _____ a stomachache.

4. She _____ an earache. She _____ a cough.

5. He _____ a stomachache. He _____ a sore throat.

Grammar to Communicate 2:
Simple Present: *Yes / No* Questions with *Have, Feel, Need, Want*

A Complete the conversations. Use *do, does, don't,* and *doesn't*. Use capital letters as needed.

1. **A:** _____Do_____ you feel OK?

    B: No, I _____. I have a fever.

2. **A:** _____ Rafael feel OK?

    B: No, he _____.

3. **A:** _____ the children have colds?

    B: No, they _____.

4. **A:** _____ Mia have the flu?

    B: Yes, she _____.

5. **A:** _____ you want water?

    B: Yes, I _____.

6. **A:** _____ Ann feel better?

    B: Yes, she _____.

B Complete the questions. Use the correct forms of *do, feel,* or *have*. Then look at the list. Answer the questions. Use short answers.

NAME	PROBLEM
Teresa	nauseous
Bill	a headache
Jack	dizzy
Cora and Tim	stomachaches
Jane and Ted	the flu

1. **A:** _____Does_____ Teresa _____feel_____ nauseous?

    B: Yes, she does. _____.

2. **A:** _____ Cora and Tim _____ stomachaches?

    B: _____.

3. **A:** _____ Jack a fever?

    B: _____. He _____ dizzy.

4. **A:** _____ Jane and Ted _____ the flu?

    B: _____.

5. **A:** _____ Bill _____ a fever?

    B: _____. He _____ a headache.

NAME: _____   DATE: _____

Review

Write *Yes / No* questions with the verbs *feel* or *have*. Then look at the pictures and answer the questions.

1. A: _____Does she have_____ a headache?

   B: _No, she doesn't. She has a backache._

2. A: _____ dizzy?

   B: _____

3. A: _____ sick?

   B: _____

4. A: _____ sore throats?

   B: _____

5. A: _____ coughs?

   B: _____

UNIT 11 VOCABULARY EXERCISES

 A   CompleteComplete the story. Use the words in the box.

brushes his teeth	do the dishes	gets home	goes to work
checks e-mail	eats breakfast	~~gets up~~	takes a shower
cooks dinner	gets dressed	goes to bed	works

Matthew Lee _____*gets up*_____ at 6:30 A.M. He goes to the
               1.

bathroom and _____. He likes the hot water. Then
               2.

he _____. He wears pants, a shirt, and a tie. At 7:15,
     3.

he goes to the kitchen. He _____ and drinks coffee.
               4.

Then he _____ in the bathroom. At 7:45, Matthew
       5.

_____. He _____ from 8:00 to 5:00.
   6.   **7.**

His house is near the office. He _____ at 5:30. Matthew
               8.

goes to the computer and _____. Matthew lives with
               9.

his mother. His mother _____ in the evening. The
               10.

food is good. Matthew eats dinner with his mother. After dinner, they

_____ in the kitchen. Matthew reads books and listens to
   11.

music. At 10:30 P.M., he _____.
              12.

B **Complete each sentence. Circle the letter of the correct answer.**

1. Mr. and Mrs. Kim often go to New York. They _____ .

   a. play cards   **(b.)** visit friends

2. Maria likes music. She often _____ on Saturday nights.

   a. plays soccer   **b.** goes dancing

3. Jean-Paul and his wife usually _____ from 8:00 to 10:00. Then they go to bed.

   a. play soccer   **b.** watch TV

4. Mr. and Mrs. Olin are at the movie theater. They always _____ on Sunday afternoon.

   a. go to the movies   **b.** go shopping

5. The students go to school from 8:00 to 3:00. At 3:30, they have fun. They _____ .

   a. play soccer   **b.** go to bed

6. Nancy and Beatriz like Chinese food. They don't like to cook. They usually _____ on Saturdays.

   a. eat out   **b.** relax

7. Tina loves clothes. She _____ every Saturday.

   a. eats out   **b.** goes shopping

8. Eriko likes movies. She always _____ on Friday night.

   a. gets a DVD   **b.** plays soccer

9. Dalal doesn't relax on Saturday and Sunday. He _____ .

   a. plays cards   **b.** works

10. Mrs. Hillman likes to _____ with her three friends in the evening. She always stays home at night.

   a. eat out   **b.** play cards

UNIT 11 GRAMMAR EXERCISES

Grammar to Communicate 1:
Simple Present: Adverbs of Frequency

A Write sentences. Put the words in the correct order.

1. I sometimes take a shower at 10:00 P.M.
    (10:00 P.M. / a / sometimes / I / take / at / shower)

2. _____
    (never / He / late / gets / home)

3. _____
    (6:00 / mother / dinner / always / My / at / cooks)

4. _____
    (children / never / dishes / The / do / the)

5. _____
    (sometimes / We / late / to / go / bed)

6. _____
    (at / sister / checks / always / My / e-mail / night)

B Look at Tom's schedule. Then write sentences about Tom. Use *never*, *sometimes*, or *always* and the correct form of the verb.

Tom's Schedule	Monday	Tuesday	Wednesday	Thursday	Friday
eat breakfast					
go to work at 8:00 A.M.	✓	✓	✓	✓	✓
get home at 5:00 P.M.			✓	✓	
cook dinner	✓	✓	✓	✓	✓
go to bed at 11:00 P.M.		✓			✓
take a shower at night					

1. Tom never eats breakfast.

2. _____

3. _____

4. _____

5. _____

6. _____

Grammar to Communicate 2:
Simple Present: Information Questions

A Complete each question. Use a form of *do* and the words in parentheses.

1. How often ____*does*____ your brother _____*play soccer*_____?
    (play soccer)

2. When _____ you _____?
    (go shopping)

3. What time _____ they _____?
    (go dancing)

4. When _____ your mother _____?
    (relax)

5. Where _____ Jenna _____?
    (play cards)

6. How often _____ your parents _____?
    (go to the movies)

7. When _____ Mr. Soto _____?
    (visit his parents)

B Read each question. Circle the letter of the correct answer to the question.

1. How often do you go shopping?
    a. Every weekend.   **b.** At 5:00.

2. Does she play cards?
    a. Yes, she does.   **b.** On Tuesday evenings.

3. What time does he go dancing?
    a. At 11:00 P.M.   **b.** On Saturdays.

4. Do they watch TV?
    a. Yes, they do.   **b.** At night.

5. When do you go to the movies?
    a. Always.   **b.** On Saturdays.

6. How often do they eat out?
    a. Every Saturday night.   **b.** Tuesdays.

7. Where does Sara play video games?
    a. At Miguel's house.   **b.** On weekends.

Review

Match the questions with the answers. Write the correct letters.

_d_ **1.** When do you get up?

____ **2.** Do you eat breakfast?

____ **3.** When do you leave the house?

____ **4.** Where do you work?

____ **5.** When do you eat lunch?

____ **6.** And where do you eat lunch?

____ **7.** When do you get home?

____ **8.** What do you do on the weekend?

____ **9.** How often do you play?

a. I eat lunch in the park.

b. Every Saturday.

c. I often play soccer or basketball.

d. I get up at 7:00.

e. Yes. I always eat breakfast in the morning.

f. I always eat lunch at 12:00.

g. I always get home at 6:00. I never work late.

h. I always leave for work at 8:00 A.M.

i. I work at a bank.

NAME: _____   DATE: _____

UNIT 12 VOCABULARY EXERCISES

A **Complete each sentence. Use the words in the box.**

coffee shop	hospital	movie theater	parking lot
department store	~~library~~	park	

1. Books are in the ___library___.

2. The students always play soccer in the _____.

3. There is coffee, tea, and hot chocolate at the _____.

4. Cars are in the _____.

5. Dresses, suits, and shoes are in the _____.

6. There is a good movie at the _____.

7. Doctors are in the _____.

B **Match the sentences. Write the correct letters.**

__d__ 1. Is there a good place to eat near here?

____ 2. I need a place to live.

____ 3. I need gas.

____ 4. I need money.

____ 5. I need help.

____ 6. Please mail this today. It's important.

a. There's a gas station on First Street.

b. There's an apartment building on Main Street.

c. OK. There's a post office on the corner.

d. Go to Marie's Restaurant.

e. Call 911. They call the police station and the firehouse.

f. There's a bank on Park Avenue.

C **Complete each conversation. Circle the correct answer.**

1. **Mom:** Brush your teeth.

   Eddie: Where's the (toothpaste) / soap?

2. **Nadia:** What's for breakfast?

   Dad: We have **milk and cookies / eggs and fruit.**

3. **Mom:** Take a shower.

   Eddie: Where's the **soap / fish?**

4. **Franco:** I need toothpaste and soap.

   Mei-Ling: There's a **drugstore / hospital** near here.

5. **Ulla:** I need fish and vegetables.

   Xan: There's a **convenience store / grocery store** on Willow Avenue.

6. **Gong:** I need a T-shirt.

   Karen: Go to a **discount store / supermarket.**

7. **Sam:** There's a convenience store!

   David: Good. I want **milk and cookies / meat and vegetables.**

8. **Lourdes:** (*on her cell phone*) Hi, Carlos. I'm at the **supermarket / drugstore.** What do you want for dinner?

   Carlos: Chicken and vegetables.

NAME: _____   DATE: _____

UNIT 12 GRAMMAR EXERCISES

Grammar to Communicate 1:
Prepositions of Location

 A   Look at the picture. Match the beginnings of the sentences with the endings.

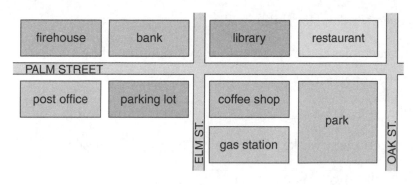

___d___ **1.** The bank is on the corner of   a. the post office.

_____ **2.** The post office is on   b. Elm Street.

_____ **3.** The firehouse is next to   c. the firehouse.

_____ **4.** The gas station is on   d. Palm Street and Elm Street.

_____ **5.** The park is across from   e. the bank.

_____ **6.** The parking lot is next to   f. Palm Street.

_____ **7.** The restaurant is on the corner of g. Palm Street and Oak Street.

_____ **8.** The post office is across from   h. the restaurant.

B   Look again at the picture in Exercise A. Complete the sentences. Use *on, on the corner of, next to,* and *across from*.

1. The coffee shop is ___next to___ the gas station.

2. The library is _____ Palm Street and Elm Street.

3. The restaurant is _____ the library.

4. The park is _____ Palm Street and Oak Street.

5. The bank is _____ the library.

6. The firehouse is _____ Palm Street.

7. The parking lot is _____ the coffee shop.

Grammar to Communicate 2:
Object Pronouns: *It* and *Them*

A Complete each sentence. Use *it* or *them*.

1. I love <u>fruit</u>. I eat _____ it _____ every day.

2. She cooks <u>fish</u> every Friday. Her children like _____.

3. We usually buy <u>vegetables</u> at the grocery store. We sometimes buy _____ at the supermarket.

4. My daughter likes <u>eggs</u>. I cook _____ every Saturday morning.

5. They eat <u>hamburgers</u> every weekend. They buy _____ on sale.

6. My children don't like <u>meat</u>. We never eat _____.

7. <u>Spaghetti</u> is his favorite food. He eats _____ three times a week.

B Complete each sentence. Use *it* or *them*.

1. We need toothpaste. Please buy _____ it _____ at the discount store.

2. You eat a lot of fish. Where do you buy _____?

3. There's no milk. We need _____ for breakfast.

4. I want some fruit. I love _____.

5. I don't want any eggs. I don't like _____.

6. Please pass the turkey sandwiches. I really like _____.

7. We eat tacos every Friday. The kids love _____.

8. Jack always cooks the meat. He cooks _____ really well.

Review

Look at the map. Complete the conversations. Use *it, them, on, on the corner of,* *across from,* **or** *next to.*

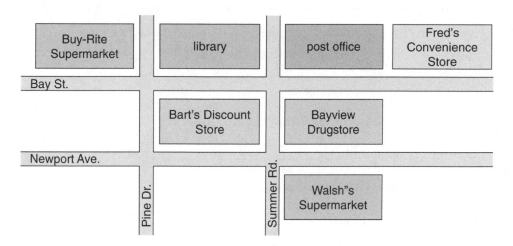

1. **A:** We need vegetables. Where do you usually buy ___them___?

   B: At Walsh's Supermarket. It's ___on___ Newport Avenue.

2. **A:** We need meat. Where do you usually buy _____?

   B: Buy-Rite Supermarket has good meat. It's _____ Bay Street and Pine Drive.

3. **A:** We have no soap. Where do you usually get _____?

   B: I usually get soap at Bart's Discount Store. It's _____ the library.

4. **A:** We need cookies for the party. Where does Mom buy _____?

   B: She usually buys cookies at Fred's Convenience Store. It's _____ the post office.

5. **A:** I need toothpaste. Where do you buy _____?

   B: I usually buy toothpaste at Bayview Drugstore. It's _____ Summer Road.

UNIT 13 VOCABULARY EXERCISES

A   **Complete the story. Use the words in the box.**

drinks coffee	listens to music	reads	studies	watches
helps	plays	~~sleeps~~	talks on the phone	

Ruth and Richard are sister and brother. On weekends, Ruth gets up at

7:00 A.M. Richard doesn't get up at 7:00. He _____*sleeps*_____ until

                                   1.

11:00. Ruth drinks milk for breakfast, but Richard _____.

                                             2.

He likes it with milk and sugar. Ruth always _____ the

                                          3.

newspaper, but Richard doesn't. He _____ TV. Ruth

                                           4.

often _____ at the library, but Richard doesn't. He

                    5.

_____ video games. Ruth _____.

                 6.   **7.**

She likes Mozart and Beethoven. Richard has a cell phone. He

_____ all day. Ruth _____ her friends

                   8.   **9.**

with their homework. Richard never studies. Who needs Ruth's help? Richard

does!

B **Complete the story. Use the words in the box.**

clean	fixes the door	takes care of
do homework	gets the mail	takes out
does the laundry	makes	watches the children

Mr. and Mrs. Santiago have two children. Their names are Ana and

Victor. The parents work during the day. The children get home from school

at 3:00. Wendy is Mrs. Santiago's friend. She _____

1.

from 3:00 to 6:00. Wendy helps the children with English, math, and

science. The children _____. When they have questions,

2.

they ask Wendy. After homework, Wendy and the children help with the

housework. They _____ the house. Ana gets water

3.

and _____ the plants. Victor cleans his bedroom and

4.

_____ his bed. Sometimes Wendy _____

5. 6.

if there are no clean clothes. Mrs. Santiago gets home at 6:00. She

_____. Sometimes there's a letter from her family in Peru.

7.

At 6:30, Mr. Santiago gets home. They have dinner. After dinner, Ana helps her

mother do the dishes. Victor _____ the trash. "Dad," says

8.

Victor. "The door doesn't close."

"OK," answers Mr. Santiago. Mr. Santiago _____. "It's

9.

OK now."

UNIT 13 GRAMMAR EXERCISES

Grammar to Communicate I:
Present Progressive: Affirmative Statements

A **Complete each sentence. Use the verbs in parentheses. Use contractions.**

1. Jackie is in her room. She <u>'s studying</u>.
   (study)

2. The boys are in the living room. They _____ video games.
   (play)

3. Please be quiet. Your father _____.
   (sleep)

4. I'm in the kitchen. I _____ on the phone.
   (talk)

5. Don is in the dining room. He _____ the newspaper.
   (read)

6. Alyssa and Joan are in the kitchen. They _____ coffee.
   (drink)

B **Complete the conversations. Use the words in the box. Use contractions.**

check	play	read	study	talk	~~watch~~

1. **A:** Where's Mom?

   B: She's in her bedroom. She <u>'s watching</u> a movie.

2. **A:** Where are your brothers?

   B: They're in the living room. They _____ video games.

3. **A:** Where's Max?

   B: He's at the library. He _____ for a test.

4. **A:** Where are your grandparents?

   B: They're in the living room. They _____ the newspaper.

5. **A:** Where are Tara and Jillian?

   B: They're in their bedroom. They _____ on their cell phones.

6. **A:** Where's Eric?

   B: He's in the living room. He _____ e-mail.

Grammar to Communicate 2
Present Progressive: Negative Statements

A Read the sentence. Write a negative statement. Use the words in parentheses.

1. She's reading the newspaper.

   She isn't studying.
   (study)

2. He's cleaning the kitchen.

   _____
   (do the laundry)

3. The children are making their beds.

   _____
   (play video games)

4. Rebecca and Shari are listening to music.

   _____
   (talk on the phone)

5. Ms. Santelli is watching TV.

   _____
   (do the dishes)

6. Rita and Maria are doing homework.

   _____
   (watch TV)

B Look at the pictures. Then read the sentences. The sentences aren't true. Write two true sentences.

1. They're doing the dishes.

   They aren't doing the dishes.

   They're taking out the trash.

2. She's reading the newspaper.

   _____

   _____

3. He's fixing the door.

   _____

   _____

4. They're checking e-mail.

   _____

   _____

Review

Complete the chart with the correct words.

Full Form	Contractions	Negative with Contractions
I am _studying_.	_I'm_ studying.	I'm not _____.
You are studying.	_____ studying.	You _____ studying.
He is _____.	_____ studying.	He isn't _____.
She is studying.	_____ studying.	She _____ studying.
We are _____.	_____ studying.	We _____ studying.
They are studying.	They're _____.	They _____ studying.

UNIT 14 VOCABULARY EXERCISES

A **Complete each conversation. Use the words in the box.**

cross the street	park the car	take a taxi	~~take the subway~~	wait for the light
drive	ride my bike	take the bus	take the train	walk

1. **Sam:** Do you usually ____take the subway____ in Paris?

   Jean: Yes, the metro is very good. I don't need a car.

2. **Sam:** How do you get to school?

   Student: I always _____. I sit with my friends. We talk. It's fun.

3. **Sam:** How do you get to the post office?

   Mrs. Lee: I _____. It's across the street!

4. **Sam:** How do you get to the airport?

   Mr. Boulet: I always _____. I don't use my car. Airport parking is $15.00 a day!

5. **Sam:** How do you get to the park?

   Rob: I _____. It's nice on a sunny day.

6. **Sam:** How do you get from Boston to New York?

   Ms. Wang: I _____. I don't like airplanes, and I don't drive.

7. **Sam:** How do you get to work?

   Karen: I usually _____ my car. I _____ in the parking lot.

8. **Sam:** How do you get to school?

   Susie: I walk with my mom. When the light is red, we _____. When the light is green, we _____.

B **Match the beginnings of the sentences with the endings. Write the correct letters.**

_c_ **1.** It's time to go to school. Get in

____ **2.** We're here. Get out of

____ **3.** Don't get on

____ **4.** When you cross the street, get off

a. your bike and walk.

b. this subway. We want the Blue line. This is the Red line.

c. the car. We're late.

d. the taxi. Give the driver his money.

C **Match the sentences with the pictures. Write the correct letters.**

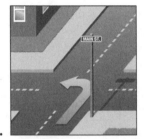
a.

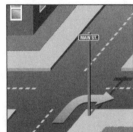
b.

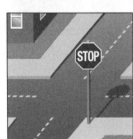
c.

d.

_c_ **1.** Stop!

____ **2.** Go straight.

____ **3.** Turn left.

____ **4.** Turn right.

UNIT 14 GRAMMAR EXERCISES

Grammar to Communicate 1:
Present Progressive: *Yes / No* Questions and Short Answers

A Write *yes / no* questions. Put the words in correct order. Use capital letters as needed.

1. Is Jose waiting for the light? _____
   (Jose / wait for the light)

2. _____
   (the children / cross the street)

3. _____
   (the teacher / take the bus to school)

4. _____
   (we / walk to the store)

5. _____
   (Mr. and Mrs. Clinton / drive to the park)

6. _____
   (your sister / ride her bike)

7. _____
   (Jessica / take the train to the city)

8. _____
   (Sun and Min Yung / drive to school)

B Complete the conversations. Use the words in parentheses.

1. **A:** _____Is_____ Babs ____taking the bus to work____?
                              (take the bus to work)

   B: Yes, _____she is_____.

2. **A:** _____ Jack and Jill _____?
                                        (drive to school)

   B: No, _____. They're taking the bus.

3. **A:** _____ Mr. Rios _____?
                                  (walk to work)

   B: No, _____. He's driving.

4. **A:** _____ the children _____?
                                      (ride their bikes to school)

   B: Yes, _____.

5. **A:** _____ you _____?
                              (take a taxi to work)

   B: No, _____. I'm taking the train.

6. **A:** _____ he _____?
                            (park the car)

   B: Yes, _____.

Grammar to Communicate 2:
Present Progressive: Information Questions

A   Write questions. Put the words in the correct order. Use capital letters as needed.

1. _Where is Mr. Chappel going?_ _____
    (Mr. Chappel / going / where / is)

2. _____
    (Carla / what / waiting / for / is)

3. _____
    (Bonnie / turning / is / where)

4. _____
    (where / they / getting / bus / on / the / are)

5. _____
    (is / driving / who / car / the)

6. _____
    (Linda / who / talking / to / is)

B   Complete the conversations. Use the questions in the box.

> What are they doing?   Where is the train going?
>
> What is she waiting for?   Who is Mrs. Dermody talking to?
>
> Where are they going?   ~~Who is taking a taxi?~~
>
> Where is Leo going?

1. **A:** _Who is taking a taxi?_

    B: Sara's taking a taxi.

2. **A:** _____

    B: He's going to work.

3. **A:** _____

    B: They're studying for their test.

4. **A:** _____

    B: She's talking to Sam's teacher.

5. **A:** _____

    B: It's going to Boston.

6. **A:** _____

    B: She's waiting for the bus.

7. **A:** _____

    B: Paula and Tim are going to Florida.

Review

Complete the conversations. Use the words in parentheses to write questions. Look at the chart. Then answer the questions. Write complete sentences.

It's 7:00. Class is at 7:15. How are the students coming to class tonight?

	CAR	TAXI	BUS	SUBWAY	TRAIN
Cesar		✓			
Felix	✓				
Ramon			✓		
Susan				✓	
Ellen	✓				
Maria			✓		
Enrique					✓
Celia				✓	

1. A: Is Cesar driving to school? _____
        (Cesar / drive to school)
    B: No, he isn't. _____

2. A: _____
        (Who / drive to school)
    B: _____

3. A: _____
        (Enrique / take the bus)
    B: _____

4. A: _____
        (Susan and Celia / take the subway)
    B: _____

5. A: _____
        (Who / take a taxi)
    B: _____

6. A: _____
        (Who / take the bus to school tonight)
    B: _____

UNIT 15 VOCABULARY EXERCISES

A   **Complete each sentence. Use the words in the box.**

bake	draw	paints	sew	tell jokes
dance	knit	plays the guitar	~~sing~~	work in her garden

1. Kentaro and Hiro like karaoke. They like to _____sing_____.

2. Gemma likes to take care of plants. She likes to _____.

3. Becky makes apple pie and chocolate cake. She likes to _____.

4. Mother is making a sweater. She likes to _____.

5. Carlos and Beatriz like salsa music. They like to _____.

6. Mrs. Brown makes dresses. She likes to _____.

7. The children have red, blue, green, and yellow pencils. They like to

   _____.

8. Theo likes rock music. He _____.

9. Xu is funny. He likes to _____.

10. Ellen is a good painter. She _____ beautiful pictures.

B **Complete each sentence. Use the words in the box.**

an airport	a factory	a nursery	a pet shop
a daycare center	a hotel	an office	

1. My daughter is three years old. She goes to _____ in the morning.

2. My father makes cars. He works at _____ in our city.

3. The Matsui family wants a dog. They go to _____.

4. Bob takes care of plants. He works at _____.

5. Mr. and Mrs. Kim are visiting London. They are staying at _____ for a week.

6. Paulo works for Brazil Air. He works at _____.

7. Lenore works in New York. She has a desk by a window. She uses a computer all day. She works in _____.

UNIT 15 GRAMMAR EXERCISES

Grammar to Communicate 1:
Can **for Ability: Statements**

A   **Complete each sentence. Use** *can* **and the verbs in parentheses.**

1. Steven is a very good cook. He ___can cook___ delicious French food.
    (cook)

2. Mary is a great dancer. She _____ flamenco.
    (dance)

3. Andy always fixes things in our house. He _____ sinks,
    (fix)
    and doors and windows.

4. I always help around the house. I _____ the laundry
    (do)
    and make the beds.

5. The children are good artists. They _____ nice pictures.
    (draw)

6. We love guitar music. We _____ the guitar really well.
    (play)

B   **Read each sentence. Then write a new sentence. Use** *can* **or** *can't* **and the**
    verbs in the box. You may use some verbs more than one time.

| ~~cook~~   draw   drive   ~~fix~~   paint   play   sew   sing |

1. Luis is a very good cook, but he's not good with machines.

    Luis ___can cook___, but he ___can't fix___ things.

2. Marta is a bad painter, but she sews beautiful clothes.

    Marta _____, but she _____.

3. I'm a terrible baseball player, but I'm a good soccer player.

    I _____ baseball, but I _____ soccer.

4. My sister doesn't sing very well, but she's a good dancer.

    My sister _____, but she _____.

5. Jake is a talented artist, but he's a terrible driver.

    Jake _____, but he _____ very well.

Grammar to Communicate 2:
Can for Ability: *Yes / No* Questions
Can: Information Questions

A Complete the conversations. Put the words in the correct order. Write questions with *can*. Then complete the answers.

1. **A:** <u>Can Manny work on Sundays?</u>
   (Manny / work on Sundays)
   B: No, _____ he can't _____.

2. **A:** _____
   (you / cook Italian food)
   B: Yes, _____.

3. **A:** _____
   (Ms. Ramirez / drive a car)
   B: Yes, _____.

4. **A:** _____
   (they / take care of animals)
   B: Yes, _____.

5. **A:** _____
   (you / start work tonight)
   B: No, _____.

6. **A:** _____
   (the students / fix computers)
   B: No, _____.

B   **Complete the conversations. Read the answers. Write questions with *When*, *Where*, or *What*. Use *can* and the verbs in parentheses.**

1. **A:** <u>When can you work?</u>_____
                                    (work)
    B: I can work Monday and Wednesday afternoons.

2. **A:** _____
                                    (do)
    B: She can use a computer, and she can speak Spanish.

3. **A:** _____
                                    (work)
    B: He can work in a hospital or daycare center.

4. **A:** _____
                                    (start)
    B: They can start on Monday.

5. **A:** _____
                                    (do)
    B: She can take care of animals.

6. **A:** _____
                                    (do)
    B: I can sing and dance, and I can play the guitar.

Review

Look at the chart. Complete the conversation.

What can you do?	
Use a computer	✓
Write in English	✓
Fix computers	✗
Drive a car	✓
Take care of children	✗

When can you work?		
	Day	Night
Monday	✓	✗
Tuesday	✗	✓
Wednesday	✓	✗
Thursday	✗	✓
Friday	✗	✓
Saturday	✗	✗
Sunday	✗	✗

A: Can you use a computer?

B: _____Yes_____, I _____can_____.

A: Can you write in English?

B: _____, I _____.

A: Can you fix computers?

B: _____, I _____.

A: Can you drive a car?

B: _____, I _____.

A: Can you work on Mondays during the day?

B: _____, I _____.

A: When can you work nights?

B: I _____ _____ on _____,

_____, and _____ nights.

A: Can you work weekends?

B: _____, I _____.

UNIT 16 VOCABULARY EXERCISES

A Read each conversation on the left. Where are the people? Match the conversations with the sentences. Write the correct letters.

_d_ **1. Jessica:** I want to watch TV.

    Henry: OK. I'm making cookies in the kitchen.

_____ **2. Sun-mi:** Look at these dresses!

    Paula: And these shoes! I want to go into this store.

_____ **3. Ms. Kaye:** Take out your homework

    Juan: Psst! Luis! Do you have a pencil?

_____ **4. Sylvia:** Look at her white dress! It's beautiful!

    Nestor: They look very happy. They're in love.

_____ **5. Liz:** Do you have the tickets?

    Hector: Yes. Do you want some soda or chocolate?

    Liz: Sure.

_____ **6. Mr. Dean:** Hi, Joe. This is Julio. He's new at the factory. Can he watch you today?

    Joe: Sure. You can help me, too, Julio.

    Julio: Thanks.

_____ **7. Sam and Ed:** We're very sick.

    Doctor: You have the flu. It's very serious.

    Sam and Ed: Can we go home?

    Mom: No, you can't. You're staying here.

_____ **8. Eva:** The water is beautiful—so blue and cool!

    Antonio: I love the warm weather.

    Eva: Yeah! No sweaters, no suits, and no shoes!

_____ **9. Jun:** I don't need my cell phone.

    Xan: And I don't need to check my e-mail.

    Jun and Xan: No work for two weeks!

_____ **10. Gina:** Hawaii is beautiful. I love you.

    Andrew: I love you, too.

a. They're in school.

b. They're at the movies.

c. They're on vacation.

d. They're at home.

e. They're at work.

f. They're at the mall.

g. They're at a wedding.

h. They're on their honeymoon.

i. They're at the beach.

j. They're in the hospital.

B Look at last year's calendar for the month of January. Answer the questions. Write the dates.

January						
1 New Year's Day	2 Jim on vacation	3	4	5	6	7 →
8 Pierre goes to Paris	9	10	11	12	13	14 →
15 Jim's birthday	16 Carol goes to doctor	17 dance class	18	19 dance class	20	21
22 Mom's birthday	23 no school	24 dance class	25	26 dance class	27 Grandma visits	28 →
29 →	30	31 dance class				

1. When was New Year's?   January first

2. When was Jim on vacation?   _____

3. When was Pierre in Paris?   _____

4. When was Carol at the doctor? _____

5. When was dance class?   _____

6. When was Jim's birthday?   _____

7. When was Mom's birthday?   _____

8. When was Grandma visiting?   _____

9. When was there no school?   _____

C **Write the dates.**

1. 3/6 = <u>March sixth</u>

2. 5/21 = _____

3. 1/30 = _____

4. 8/16 = _____

5. 12/25 = _____

6. 9/10 = _____

7. 2/1 = _____

8. 4/2 = _____

9. 10/3 = _____

10. 6/24 = _____

11. 11/20 = _____

12. 7/12 = _____

UNIT 16 GRAMMAR EXERCISES

Grammar to Communicate 1:
Simple Past of *Be*: Statements

A **Complete each sentence. Use *was* or *were*.**

1. I _____was_____ on vacation in California last week.

2. Yuko _____ at the movies last night.

3. Bonita and Jose _____ at a party last Saturday.

4. The children _____ in school yesterday.

5. We _____ on our honeymoon last month.

6. Mr. Robles _____ in the hospital last night.

7. My daughter _____ at the mall yesterday.

8. They _____ at the beach on Saturday.

B **Look at Vicky's planner from last week. Complete each sentence. Use *was* or *wasn't*.**

SUN.	MON.	TUES.	WED.	THURS.	FRI.	SAT.
beach	work	work	doctor's appt.	school	movies	clean apt.

1. Vicky ____wasn't____ at work on Sunday. She ____was____ at the beach.

2. Vicky _____ at work on Tuesday.

3. Vicky _____ at the doctor's office on Wednesday.

4. Vicky _____ at work on Thursday. She _____ in school.

5. On Friday night, Vicky _____ at the movies. She _____ in school.

6. On Saturday, Vicky _____ at home. She _____ at the beach.

Grammar to Communicate 2:
Simple Past of *Be*: *Yes* / *No* Questions and Short Answers
Simple Past of *Be*: *Wh-* Questions

A Complete the conversations. Write questions. Put the words in the correct order. Then complete the answers. Use capital letters as needed.

1. **A:** _Were James and Tony in school last year?_____
       (year / last / James and Tony / were / school / in)
    B: Yes, _____ they were _____.

2. **A:** _____
       (Mr. Crawley / in / was / Argentina / July / in)
    B: No, _____.

3. **A:** _____
       (they / school / in / were / on / June 15 / year / last)
    B: Yes, _____.

4. **A:** _____
       (you / vacation / month / were / last / on)
    B: No, _____.

5. **A:** _____
       (he / yesterday / work / at / was)
    B: Yes, _____.

6. **A:** _____
       (Ms. Collins and Mr. Pappas / Florida / were / in / week / last)
    B: No, _____.

B Read the answers. Then complete the questions. Use *Who*, *Where*, *When*, *Why*, and *How*.

1. **A:** _____Where_____ were you yesterday?

    B: I was at home.

2. **A:** _____ was Ms. Franco in Spain?

    B: She was there in 1999.

3. **A:** _____ was she there?

    B: It was her brother's wedding.

4. **A:** _____ was she there with?

    B: She was there with her sister.

5. **A:** _____ was your vacation?

    B: It was great!

6. **A:** _____ was the party?

    B: It was on the fifteenth.

7. **A:** _____ was there?

    B: My friends from work and some neighbors were there.

8. **A:** _____ was the party?

    B: It was at Miguel's house.

Review

Complete the conversation. Use the questions in the box.

How long were you in San Francisco?	Were you in a hotel?
How was the weather?	Where was that?
~~How was your vacation?~~	Where were you again?
Were you at work on the eleventh?	Who were you with?

A: <u>How was your vacation?</u>

B: It was really great.

A: _____

B: We were in San Francisco.

A: _____ It can be cold in San Francisco.

B: The weather was perfect. It was cool at night, but during the day it was warm.

A: _____

B: Yes, we were. Our hotel was right in Union Square.

A: _____

B: My parents. And my sister was there, too.

A: _____

B: We were there for five days. We left on the tenth.

A: _____

B: No, I wasn't. I was at my parents' house for three days.

A: _____

B: In Chicago. I was back at home last night.

Unit 1, page 1, vocabulary

A

2. Ms. Susan Gray
3. Mr. Tanner, Charles
4. Ms. Wong, Grace

B

2. Bibi	11. Karen	20. Theo
3. Carlos	12. Lourdes	21. Ulla
4. Dalal	13. Mpholo	22. Victor
5. Eva	14. Nadia	23. Walo
6. Ferenc	15. Oriana	24. Xan
7. Gong	16. Pierre	25. Yolanda
8. Hi-won	17. Quincy	26. Zina
9. Ilhan	18. Ruth	
10. Jun	19. Sun-mi	

Unit 1, page 3, grammar

Grammar to Communicate 1

A

2. My first name is Maria.
3. It's nice to meet you.
4. I am Tom Baker.
5. My last name is Lee.
6. Please call me Nora.

B

2. is
3. nice
4. 'm
5. It's
6. My

Grammar to Communicate 2

A

2. He
3. His
4. His
5. She
6. Her

B

2. e
3. c
4. a
5. b

Review

B: Hello. My name is Beth Green. What's your last name again?

A: Franklin. Jim Franklin. It's nice to meet you, Ms. Green.

B: It's nice to meet you, Mr. Franklin. And please call me Beth.

A: And please call me Jim.

Unit 2, page 6, vocabulary

A

1. Canada	8. Germany	14. India
3. Mexico	9. France	15. China
4. Peru	10. Spain	16. Taiwan
5. Brazil	11. Italy	17. Korea
6. Ireland	12. Somalia	18. Japan
7. England	13. Russia	

B

2. Spanish	5. Chinese	8. German
3. Japanese	6. Mexican	9. Korean
4. Italian	7. British	

Unit 2, page 9, grammar

Grammar to Communicate 1

A

2. I'm Alfredo.
3. He's my teacher.
4. She's cute.
5. They're from France.
6. We're from Taiwan.
7. You're from the U.S.
8. It's Italian.

B

2. Anna's not / Anna is not from Germany.
3. Mr. Solomon's not / Mr. Solomon is not from Canada.
4. We're / We are not from Italy.
5. They're / They are not from India.
6. Tacos aren't / are not from Brazil.

Grammar to Communicate 2

A

2. Are you French?
3. Are they Japanese?
4. Are you Canadian?
5. Is he British?
6. Are Sara and Maria from Spain?

B

2. Jack and Sam aren't British.
3. Lucy isn't from Canada. / Lucy's not from Canada.
4. The teacher isn't Japanese. / The teacher's not Japanese.
5. I'm not from France.
6. Wendy and I aren't from India.

Answer Key

Review

B: No, they **aren't**. They're German.

A: **Are** French fries American?

B: No, they aren't. **They're** from Belgium.

A: Is spaghetti American?

B: No, it **isn't**. It's Italian.

A: **Is** fried chicken American?

B: Yes, it **is**.

Unit 3, page 12, vocabulary

A

2. 4	5. 6	8. 5
3. 7	6. 3	9. 8
4. 2	7. 9	

B

2. 9	7. 13	12. 1	17. 19
3. 11	8. 4	13. 14	18. 17
4. 2	9. 5	14. 8	19. 6
5. 10	10. 0	15. 16	20. 15
6. 12	11. 3	16. 7	

Unit 3, page 14, grammar

Grammar to Communicate 1

A

2. a
3. an
4. a
5. a
6. an

B

1. a
2. a, a
3. a, a
4. a, an
5. a, a
6. an, an

Grammar to Communicate 2

A

2. e
3. d
4. a
5. b
6. f

B

2. Where
3. What
4. How old

5. Where
6. Who

Review

B: He's my grandfather. He's **an** engineer.

A: **What's** his name?

B: His name is Thomas.

A: **Where** is he from?

B: He's from Cuba.

A: **Who's** he?

B: He's my brother. He's **a** student.

A: **What's** his name?

B: His name is Alex.

A: **How old** is he?

B: He's 16.

Unit 4, page 17, vocabulary

A

2. kblake@coolmail.com
3. 804-555-2006
4. VicSan@coolmail.com
5. 617-555-8989
6. FunSun28@coolmail.com

B

2. 53	7. 38	12. 75	17. 83
3. 24	8. 67	13. 40	18. 57
4. 99	9. 100	14. 68	
5. 85	10. 39	15. 76	
6. 21	11. 22	16. 94	

Unit 4, page 18, grammar

Grammar to Communicate 1

A

2. their
3. Their
4. Our
5. Your
6. Our

B

2. Her
3. Our
4. Your
5. His
6. Their

Grammar to Communicate 2

A

2. Mr. Roberston's cell phone number is 917-555-5993.
3. Cindy's phone number is 555-3327.

4. Mr. and Mrs. Mason's address is 5490 Port Boulevard.
5. My brother's e-mail address is gosporty@online.net.
6. Tanya's address is 320 Court Street.

B

2. His cell phone number is 917-555-5993.
3. Her phone number is 555-3327.
4. Their address is 5490 Port Boulevard.
5. His e-mail address is gosporty@online.net.
6. Her address is 320 Court Street.

Review

A: What's her **address**?
B: It's 749 Brighton Avenue.
A: What's **Sam Baer's** address?
B: It's 32 Plainfield Road.
A: What's **Bob Kane's** phone number?
B: It's 555-6673.
A: What's his address?
B: It's **3056 Ocean Boulevard**.
A: What's Julie Caruso's **address**?
B: It's 284 Rockville Street.
A: What's **her** phone number?
B: It's **555-6194**.

Unit 5, page 21, vocabulary

A

2. window
3. bookcase
4. glasses
5. eraser
6. book
7. door
8. closet
9. chair
10. notebook
11. box of chalk
12. pencil
13. pen
14. dictionary
15. desk
16. backpack
17. workbook

B

1. a
2. b
3. a

C

2. Raise
3. Open
4. Erase
5. Use
6. Read
7. Listen to
8. Write
9. Close
10. Turn to
11. Point to
12. Look at

Unit 5, page 23, grammar

Grammar to Communicate 1

A

2. The pens are on the bookcase.
3. His notebooks are in his backpack.
4. The closets are near the door.
5. Their dictionaries are on the chair.
6. The erasers are near the board.

B

2. dictionaries
3. box
4. backpack
5. workbooks
6. pen

Grammar to Communicate 2

A

2. write
3. open
4. raise
5. listen to
6. turn to
7. take out

B

2. Don't erase the board, please.
3. Don't close the door.
4. Write your answers on the paper.
5. Please look at your book.
6. Listen to me, please.

Review

3. Don't open your books.
4. Write on the answer sheet.
5. Sign the test.
6. Read all the instructions.
7. Print your name on the test.
8. Don't stand up.
9. Don't write on the test.
10. Don't talk.

Unit 6, page 26, vocabulary

A

2. cool
3. rainy
4. sunny
5. foggy
6. snowy
7. windy
8. cloudy
9. cold
10. warm

B

2. Monday
3. Tuesday
4. Wednesday
5. Thursday
6. Friday
7. Saturday

C

2. morning
3. evening
4. afternoon
5. night
6. midnight
7. noon

Answer Key

Unit 6, page 29, grammar

Grammar to Communicate 1

A

2. It's Thursday.
3. It's Tuesday.
4. It's Friday.
5. It's Wednesday.
6. It's Saturday.

B

2. e
3. b
4. d
5. a
6. f

Grammar to Communicate 2

A

2. at
3. in, to
4. on
5. at, at

B

2. What are your work hours?
3. When is their class?
4. When is the test?
5. What time is his class?
6. What time is lunch?
7. What are the office hours?

Review

2. What's / What is
3. What are
4. When's / When is
5. What time's / What time is
6. What day is
7. When are

Unit 7, page 32, vocabulary

A

2. dress, shoes
3. pants, sweater
4. jacket
5. blouse, jeans, skirt
6. suit, tie
7. pants, sneakers, T-shirt
8. jeans, polo shirt

B

1. white
2. black, red, yellow
3. green, white, red
4. red, white, blue
5. orange, purple
6. beige, brown
7. large
8. small
9. extra large
10. medium

Unit 7, page 34, grammar

Grammar to Communicate 1

A

1. those
2. This, these
3. These, those
4. This, that
5. this, Those

B

2. Those
3. That
4. this

Grammar to Communicate 2

A

2. How much are
3. How much are
4. How much is
5. How much is
6. How much are
7. How much is

B

1. **A: What color is** the shirt?
   B: It's green.
   A: How much is it?
   B: It's $19.95
2. **A: What color are** the socks?
   B: They're red.
   A: How much are they?
   B: They're **$1.99.**
3. **A: What color is** the sweater?
   B: It's blue.
   A: How much is it?
   B: It's $34.99.

Review

A: **How much is this sweater?**
B: It's $24.99.
A: That's a great price. **Are those pants on sale, too?**
B: No, those pants aren't on sale. But these pants are on sale.
A: **How much are they?**
B: They're $39.99.

A: That's good. **What color are they?**

B: They're green, black, and beige.

Unit 8, page 37, vocabulary

A

2. living room
3. children's bedroom
4. blinds
5. dining room
6. kitchen
7. parents'
8. bathroom

B

2. F
3. F
4. T
5. F
6. F
7. T
8. T

Unit 8, page 39, grammar

Grammar to Communicate 1

A

There are two large bedrooms and one small bedroom. **There are** no closets in the small bedroom. **There's** a nice living room and a small dining room. **There's** no carpeting, but **there are** blinds on all the windows. **There are** two bathrooms. **There's** one bathroom in the hall, and **there's** a bathroom in a bedroom. **There's** no air-conditioning, but **there are** seven windows.

B

2. There are two closets.
3. There are a lot of windows.
4. There are two bedrooms.
5. There's carpeting.
6. There's no dining room.
7. There's no air-conditioning.
8. There's a living room.

Grammar to Communicate 2

A

2. Is there a window in the kitchen?
3. Is there a microwave on the counter?
4. Are there any curtains on the windows?
5. Are there any cabinets over the stove?
6. Is there a table in the kitchen?
7. Are there any chairs in the kitchen?

B

A: Is there a window in the kitchen?

B: Yes, **there is**.

A: Are there any closets?

B: Yes, **there are**. There are three closets.

A: Are there any cabinets in the kitchen?

B: Yes, **there are**. There are a lot of cabinets.

A: What about the bedrooms?

B: **There are** three bedrooms—one large bedroom and two small bedrooms.

A: Is there air-conditioning?

B: No, **there isn't**.

A: Is there carpeting?

B: Yes, **there is**. There's nice blue carpeting in the living room and hall.

Review

B: Yes, **there are. / there are five closets**.

A: How's the kitchen?

B: It's very modern. There are a lot of **cabinets**.

A: **Is there** a microwave?

B: **Yes, there is**. And the stove and refrigerator are new.

A: Oh, that's great. Anything else?

B: **There's** a washing machine and dryer in the hall.

A: Is there a dining room?

B: **No, there isn't**. But **there's** a dining area in the living room.

A: That's great! And what about bathrooms?

B: There are **two** bathrooms.

A: And the bedrooms?

B: That's the best part. **There are** three bedrooms.

A: It sounds like the perfect apartment.

Unit 9, page 42, vocabulary

A

2. a
3. a
4. b
5. a
6. b
7. a

B

1. c
2. a
3. b

C

2. milk
3. juice
4. hot chocolate
5. water
6. salt
7. check
8. tea
9. iced tea
10. sugar
11. soda
12. glass
13. pepper
14. napkin

Unit 9, page 44, grammar

Grammar to Communicate 1

A

2. want
3. like
4. needs
5. need
6. wants

Answer Key

B

2. Liana wants a Swiss cheese sandwich.
3. Terry and Chris want grilled chicken sandwiches.
4. Mr. Oakes wants a salad.
5. Mindy and Carol want tomato soup.
6. Michelle wants a hamburger.

Grammar to Communicate 2

A

2. don't need
3. doesn't like
4. doesn't want
5. don't need
6. don't like

B

2. doesn't want
3. don't need
4. don't like
5. don't need
6. don't like
7. don't want
8. doesn't like

Review

2. Our teacher needs salt for his hamburger.
3. She doesn't want a salad with her lunch.
4. My children like chocolate ice cream for dessert.
5. Dave and Irene don't want more coffee.
6. Mr. Davos wants soup and a grilled chicken sandwich. / Mr. Davos wants a grilled chicken sandwich and soup.

Unit 10, page 47, vocabulary

A

2. e   3. c   4. d   5. a

B

1. d   2. c   3. a   4. b   5. e

C

1. f   4. a   7. h
2. b   5. g   8. i
3. d   6. e   9. c

Unit 10, page 49, grammar

Grammar to Communicate 1

A

2. have
3. have
4. have

5. has
6. have
7. has

B

2. has, doesn't have
3. has, doesn't have
4. doesn't have, has
5. has, doesn't have

Grammar to Communicate 2

A

1. don't
2. Does, doesn't
3. Do, don't
4. Does, does
5. Do, do
6. Does, does

B

2. **A:** Do, have
   B: Yes, they do.
3. **A:** Does, have
   B: No, he doesn't.; feels
4. **A:** Do, have
   B: Yes, they do.
5. **A:** Does, have
   B: No, he doesn't.; has

Review

2. **A:** Does she feel
   B: No, she doesn't. She feels nauseous.
3. **A:** Do they feel
   B: No, they don't. They feel tired. / Yes, they do.
4. **A:** Do they have
   B: Yes, they do.
5. **A:** Do they have
   B: No, they don't. They have stomachaches.

Unit 11, page 52, vocabulary

A

2. takes a shower
3. gets dressed
4. eats breakfast
5. brushes his teeth
6. goes to work
7. works
8. gets home
9. checks e-mail
10. cooks dinner
11. do the dishes
12. goes to bed

B

2. b   5. a   8. a
3. b   6. a   9. b
4. a   7. b   10. b

Unit 11, page 54, grammar

Grammar to Communicate 1

A

2. He never gets home late.
3. My mother always cooks dinner at 6:00.
4. The children never do the dishes.
5. We sometimes go to bed late. / Sometimes we go to bed late.
6. My sister always checks e-mail at night.

B

2. Tom / He always goes to work at 8:00 A.M.
3. Tom / He sometimes gets home at 5:00 P.M. / Sometimes Tom / he gets home at 5:00 P.M.
4. Tom / He always cooks dinner.
5. Tom / He sometimes goes to bed at 11:00 P.M. / Sometimes Tom / he goes to bed at 11:00 P.M.
6. Tom / He never takes a shower at night.

Grammar to Communicate 2

A

2. do, go shopping
3. do, go dancing
4. does, relax
5. does, play cards
6. do, go to the movies
7. does, visit his parents

B

2. a
3. a
4. a
5. b
6. a
7. a

Review

2. e
3. h
4. i
5. f
6. a
7. g
8. c
9. b

Unit 12, page 57, vocabulary

A

2. park
3. coffee shop
4. parking lot
5. department store
6. movie theater
7. hospital

B

2. b
3. a
4. f
5. e
6. c

C

2. eggs and fruit
3. soap
4. drugstore
5. grocery store
6. discount store
7. milk and cookies
8. supermarket

Unit 12, page 59, grammar

Grammar to Communicate 1

A

2. f
3. e
4. b
5. h
6. a
7. g
8. c

B

2. on the corner of
3. next to
4. on the corner of
5. across from
6. on
7. across from

Grammar to Communicate 2

A

2. it
3. them
4. them
5. them
6. it
7. it

B

2. it
3. it
4. it
5. them
6. them
7. them
8. it

Review

2. it, on the corner of
3. it, across from
4. them, next to
5. it, on

Answer Key

Unit 13, page 62, vocabulary

A

2. drinks coffee
3. reads
4. watches
5. studies
6. plays
7. listens to music
8. talks on the phone
9. helps

B

1. watches the children
2. do homework
3. clean
4. takes care of
5. makes
6. does the laundry
7. gets the mail
8. takes out
9. fixes the door

Unit 13, page 64, grammar

Grammar to Communicate 1

A

2. 're playing
3. 's sleeping.
4. 'm talking
5. 's reading
6. 're drinking

B

2. 're playing
3. 's studying
4. 're reading
5. 're talking
6. 's checking

Grammar to Communicate 2

A

2. He isn't doing the laundry.
3. The children aren't playing video games.
4. They aren't talking on the phone.
5. Ms. Santelli / She isn't doing the dishes.
6. They aren't watching TV.

B

2. She isn't reading the newspaper. She's cleaning the house.
3. He isn't fixing the door. He's fixing the sink.
4. They aren't checking e-mail. They're getting the mail.

Review

Full Form	Contractions	Negative with Contractions
I am **studying**.	**I'm** studying.	I'm not **studying**.
You are studying.	**You're** studying.	You **aren't** studying.
He is **studying**.	**He's** studying.	He isn't **studying**.
She is studying.	**She's** studying.	She **isn't** studying.
We are **studying**.	**We're** studying.	We **aren't** studying.
They are studying.	They're **studying**.	They **aren't** studying.

Unit 14, page 67, vocabulary

A

2. take the bus
3. walk
4. take a taxi
5. ride my bike
6. take the train
7. drive, park the car
8. wait for the light, cross the street

B

2. d   3. b   4. a

C

2. d   3. a   4. b

Unit 14, page 69, grammar

Grammar to Communicate 1

A

2. Are the children crossing the street?
3. Is the teacher taking the bus to school?
4. Are we walking to the store?
5. Are Mr. and Mrs. Clinton driving to the park?
6. Is your sister riding her bike?
7. Is Jessica taking the train to the city?
8. Are Sun and Min Yung driving to school?

B

2. **A:** Are, driving to school
   B: they aren't / they're not
3. **A:** Is, walking to work
   B: he isn't / he's not

4. **A:** Are, riding their bikes to school
   B: they are
5. **A:** Are, taking a taxi to work
   B: I'm not
6. **A:** Is, parking the car
   B: he is

Grammar to Communicate 2

A

2. What is Carla waiting for?
3. Where is Bonnie turning?
4. Where are they getting on the bus?
5. Who is driving the car?
6. Who is Linda talking to?

B

2. Where is Leo going?
3. What are they doing?
4. Who is Mrs. Dermody talking to?
5. Where is the train going?
6. What is she waiting for?
7. Where are they going?

Review

2. **A:** Who's driving to school?
   B: Felix and Ellen are driving to school.
3. **A:** Is Enrique taking the bus?
   B: No, he isn't / he's not. (He's taking the train.)
4. **A:** Are Susan and Celia taking the subway?
   B: Yes, they are.
5. **A:** Who's taking a taxi?
   B: Cesar's / Cesar is taking a taxi.
6. **A:** Who's taking the bus to school tonight?
   B: Ramon and Maria are taking the bus.

Unit 15, page 72, vocabulary

A

2. work in her garden
3. bake
4. knit
5. dance
6. sew
7. draw
8. plays the guitar
9. tell jokes
10. paints

B

1. a daycare center
2. a factory
3. a pet shop
4. a nursery
5. a hotel
6. an airport
7. an office

Unit 15, page 74, grammar

Grammar to Communicate 1

A

2. can dance
3. can fix
4. can do
5. can draw
6. can play

B

2. can't paint, can sew
3. can't play, can play
4. can't sing, can dance
5. can draw / paint, can't drive

Grammar to Communicate 2

A

2. **A:** Can you cook Italian food?
   B: I can
3. **A:** Can Ms. Ramirez drive a car?
   B: she can
4. **A:** Can they take care of animals?
   B: they can
5. **A:** Can you start work tonight?
   B: I can't
6. **A:** Can the students fix computers?
   B: they can't

B

2. What can she do?
3. Where can he work?
4. When can they start?
5. What can she do?
6. What can you do?

Review

B: Yes, can
B: No, I can't
B: Yes, I can.
B: Yes, I can.
B: can work, Tuesday, Thursday, Friday
B: No, I can't.

Unit 16, page 78, vocabulary

A

2. f
3. a
4. g
5. b
6. e
7. j
8. i
9. c
10. h

B

2. January second, third, fourth, fifth, sixth, and seventh
3. January eighth, ninth, tenth, eleventh, twelfth, thirteenth, and fourteenth
4. January sixteenth
5. January seventeenth, nineteenth, twenty-fourth, twenty-sixth, and thirty-first
6. January fifteenth
7. January twenty-second
8. January twenty-seventh, twenty-eighth, twenty-ninth, and thirtieth
9. January twenty-third

C

2. May twenty-first
3. January thirtieth
4. August sixteenth
5. December twenty-fifth
6. September tenth
7. February first
8. April second
9. October third
10. June twenty-fourth
11. November twentieth
12. July twelfth

Unit 16, page 81, grammar

Grammar to Communicate 1

A

2. was
3. were
4. were
5. were
6. was
7. was
8. were

B

2. was
3. was
4. wasn't, was
5. was, wasn't
6. was, wasn't

Grammar to Communicate 2

A

2. **A:** Was Mr. Crawley in Argentina in July?
   B: he wasn't
3. **A:** Were they in school on June 15 last year?
   B: they were
4. **A:** Were you on vacation last month?
   B: we weren't / I wasn't
5. **A:** Was he at work yesterday?
   B: he was
6. **A:** Were Ms. Collins and Mr. Pappas in Florida last week?
   B: they weren't

B

2. When
3. Why
4. Who
5. How
6. When
7. Who
8. Where

Review

A: Where were you again?
A: How was the weather?
A: Were you in a hotel?
A: Who were you with?
A: How long were you in San Francisco?
A: Were you at work on the eleventh?
A: Where was that?